macarons

Annie Rigg

macarons

Chic & delicious French treats

photography by Kate Whitaker

RPS

RYLAND PETERS & SMALL
LONDON • NEW YORK

Author's acknowledgments

Yet again I have had the very great pleasure of working with
Kate Whitaker and Liz Belton on this book. So here's another big
thank you to them both for their beautiful pictures and fabulous props.
And thanks to Rachel for her wonderful assistance and for endless
trays of perfect macarons. An enormous thank you to Céline and
Iona at Ryland Peters & Small for making me look good, again.
And to Holly, my neighbour, who tasted just about every recipe
in this book before declaring that macarons are 'truelly amazing!'

Senior designer Iona Hoyle
Senior editor Céline Hughes
Production Gordana Simakovic
Art director Leslie Harrington
Publishing director Alison Starling

Prop stylist Liz Belton
Indexer Hilary Bird

First published in 2011
This edition published in 2016
by Ryland Peters & Small
20–21 Jockey's Fields
London WC1R 4BW
and
341 E 116th St
New York NY 10029
www.rylandpeters.com

10 9 8 7 6 5 4 3 2 1

Text © Annie Rigg 2011, 2016
Design and photographs © Ryland Peters & Small 2011, 2016

Printed in China

ISBN: 978-1-84975-764-5

A CIP record for this book is available from the British Library.
US Library of Congress CIP data has been applied for.

Notes

° Both British (Metric) and American (Imperial plus US cups)
are included in these recipes for your convenience, however it is
important to work with one set of measurements and not alternate
between the two within a recipe.
° All spoon measurements are level unless otherwise specified.
° Eggs used in this book are UK large/US extra-large, unless
otherwise specified. Uncooked or partially cooked eggs should
not be served to the very old, frail, young children, pregnant
women or those with compromised immune systems.
° Ovens should be preheated to the specified temperatures.
All ovens work slightly differently. We recommend using an oven
thermometer and suggest you consult the maker's handbook for any
special instructions, particularly if you are cooking in a fan-assisted/
convection oven, as you will need to adjust temperatures according
to manufacturer's instructions.

Food colouring & flavouring suppliers

UK
Baker & Maker, for food colourings and sugarcraft supplies
www.bakerandmaker.com

Squires, for food colourings (pastes and powders) and various
flavouring extracts
www.squires-shop.com

US
Global Sugar Art, for cake decorating supplies
www.globalsugarart.com

France & international
French supplier, Deco relief, for concentrated liquid food flavourings
www.deco-relief.fr

contents

basic macarons

Once you've mastered this basic recipe, you can create almost any colour and flavour combination you like. You should get 40 shells – i.e. 20 filled macarons – out of all the regular-sized macaron recipes in this book.

200 g/1½ cups icing/confectioners' sugar

100 g/⅔ cup ground almonds

120–125 g/½ cup egg whites (about 3 eggs)

a pinch of salt

40 g/3 tablespoons caster/superfine sugar

a piping bag, fitted with a 1-cm/½-inch nozzle/tip

2 solid baking sheets, lined with non-stick baking parchment

1 Tip the icing/confectioners' sugar and almonds into the bowl of a food processor and blend for 30 seconds until thoroughly combined. Set aside.

2 Tip the egg whites into a spotlessly clean and dry mixing bowl. Add the salt and, using an electric handheld whisk, beat until they will only just hold a stiff peak.

3 Continue to whisk at medium speed while adding the caster/superfine sugar a teaspoonful at a time. Mix well between each addition to ensure that the sugar is thoroughly incorporated before adding the next spoonful. The mixture should be thick, white and glossy. **(a)**

4 At this point you should add any food colouring paste you are using. Dip a cocktail stick into the paste and stir into the mixture, mixing thoroughly to ensure that the colour is evenly blended. Scrape down the sides of the bowl with a rubber spatula.

e

5 Using a large metal spoon, fold the ground sugar and almond mixture into the egg whites. (**b**)

6 The mixture should be thoroughly incorporated and smooth – this can take up to 1 minute. When it is ready, the mixture should drop from the spoon in a smooth molten mass. (**c**)

7 Fill the piping bag with the mixture and pipe evenly sized rounds – about 5 cm/2 inches across – onto the prepared baking sheets. (**d**)

(If a main recipe you are following elsewhere in this book uses this Basic Macarons method, you will probably need to resume the main recipe after this step.)

8 Tap the bottom of the baking sheets sharply, once, on the work surface to expel any large air bubbles.

9 You can scatter edible decorations, liquid food colouring etc. onto the unbaked macaron shells at this stage.

10 Leave the macarons for at least 15 minutes, and up to 1 hour, until they have "set" and formed a dry shell. They should not be sticky, tacky or wet when tested with your fingertip. (**e**)

11 Preheat the oven to 170°C (325°F) Gas 3.

12 Bake the macarons on the middle shelf of the preheated oven, one sheet at a time, for 10 minutes. The tops should be crisp and the bottoms dry. Leave to cool on the baking sheet.

tips for success

° Before starting, weigh all the ingredients carefully, have them at room temperature and get your equipment ready. Cover the baking sheets neatly with baking parchment. I find that dark, solid baking sheets work better than silver-coloured ones.

° Fit your piping bag with the correct nozzle/tip. I find it easier to twist the bag just above the nozzle/tip, then put it in a bowl with the top open so that I can pour the mixture directly into the bag without using a spoon.

° If you want to be sure that every macaron shell is exactly the same size, use a cookie cutter as a guide. Draw 20 circles around the cookie cutter on each sheet of baking parchment, turn it over and pipe the macaron mixture onto each circle.

° When you have piped the rounds and tapped the baking sheets on the work surface, leave the unbaked macarons to set on a level surface for at least 15 minutes and anything up to 1 hour to dry – this is a crucial part of macaron making! It helps them to form a glossy, smooth surface and ensures that the macarons have their trademark crinkly "feet" when they come out of the oven.

° No two ovens are the same, so do adjust your oven temperature by a few degrees, or turn the baking sheets around halfway through baking if your oven cooks hotter in places.

° Once baked, cooled and filled, cover the macarons and leave in the fridge or a cool place for 30 minutes before serving.

° If your macarons aren't perfect the first time, don't give up – practice makes perfect!

traditional flavours

Once you've mastered the art and technique of simple macarons, you can let your imagination run wild with flavours and colours.

The selection of food colouring pastes now available is vast, and food colouring powders are becoming more widely available through online suppliers. Natural liquid food colours are also available in a limited selection of colours – usually red, purple, green and yellow, but the depth of colour will not be quite as vibrant as the pastes.

Natural oils and extracts are a great way of flavouring your macaron shells, and you can now find online suppliers offering quite unusual liquid flavourings such as violet and toffee apple (see page 4 for details). As with all flavourings, it's good to remember that less is more and macarons should be delicately flavoured rather than overwhelmingly so.

The flavoured macaron recipes opposite all take the Basic Macarons recipe on page 6 as their starting point.

pistachio

50 g/½ cup shelled unsalted pistachios
200 g/1½ cups icing/confectioners' sugar
75 g/½ cup ground almonds
120–125 g/½ cup egg whites (about 3 eggs)
a pinch of salt
40 g/3 tablespoons caster/superfine sugar
green food colouring paste

Use good-quality, unsalted shelled pistachios and grind them finely in a food processor along with the icing/confectioners' sugar and ground almonds in Step 1 of the Basic Macarons recipe on page 6. Add the green food colouring paste in Step 4, then continue with the recipe.

raspberry

200 g/1½ cups icing/confectioners' sugar
100 g/⅔ cup ground almonds
120–125 g/½ cup egg whites (about 3 eggs)
a pinch of salt
40 g/3 tablespoons caster/superfine sugar
raspberry flavouring
pink food colouring paste

Follow the Basic Macarons recipe on page 6. Add a little raspberry flavouring and pink food colouring paste in Step 4, then continue with the recipe. If you can't find raspberry flavouring, you can simply fill your unflavoured pink macaron shells with the very best raspberry jam.

lemon

200 g/1½ cups icing/confectioners' sugar
100 g/⅔ cup ground almonds
120–125 g/½ cup egg whites (about 3 eggs)
a pinch of salt
40 g/3 tablespoons caster/superfine sugar
1 unwaxed lemon
yellow food colouring paste

Follow the Basic Macarons recipe on page 6. Wash and dry the unwaxed lemon and finely grate the zest. Add to the macaron mixture in Step 4 with some yellow food colouring paste, then continue with the recipe. Fill the shells with delicious homemade Lemon Curd (see recipe on page 10).

chocolate

2 tablespoons good-quality cocoa powder
200 g/1½ cups icing/confectioners' sugar minus 1 tablespoon
100 g/⅔ cup ground almonds
120–125 g/½ cup egg whites (about 3 eggs)
a pinch of salt
40 g/3 tablespoons caster/superfine sugar
red food colouring paste

Put the good-quality cocoa powder in a food processor along with the icing/confectioners' sugar and ground almonds in Step 1 of the Basic Macarons recipe on page 6. Add a little red food colouring paste in Step 4 to boost the colour slightly, then continue with the recipe. Fill with Chocolate Ganache (see recipe on page 10).

fillings

chocolate ganache

150 g/5 oz. dark/bittersweet chocolate, finely chopped

150 ml/⅔ cup double/heavy cream

1 tablespoon light muscovado/light brown sugar

a pinch of salt

Put the chocolate in a small, heatproof bowl. Put the cream and sugar in a small saucepan and heat until the sugar has dissolved and the cream has come to the boil. Add the salt, then pour the hot cream over the chopped chocolate and leave to melt. Stir until smooth and leave to set and thicken slightly before using.

lemon curd

3 egg yolks

75 g/⅓ cup caster/superfine sugar

3 tablespoons unsalted butter, diced

grated zest and freshly squeezed juice of 1 unwaxed lemon

Place all the ingredients in a medium-sized heatproof bowl set over a pan of gently simmering water. Stir with a wooden spoon until the sugar has dissolved and the butter has melted. Continue to cook, stirring from time to time, until the curd has thickened and will coat the back of a spoon – this will take about 15 minutes.

Strain into a clean bowl, cover the surface with clingfilm/plastic wrap and leave to cool. Refrigerate until needed.

vanilla cream

3 egg yolks

75 g/¾ cup caster/superfine sugar

1 tablespoon cornflour/cornstarch

250 ml/1 cup full-fat milk

1 vanilla pod/bean, split lengthways

3 tablespoons unsalted butter, diced

100 ml/½ cup double/heavy cream

Put the egg yolks, sugar and cornflour/cornstarch in a small, heatproof bowl and whisk together until combined.

Heat the milk, along with the vanilla pod/bean, in a small saucepan until it only just starts to boil. Remove the vanilla and pour the hot milk over the egg mixture, whisking constantly until smooth. Pour the mixture back into the pan and cook gently over low heat, stirring constantly until the custard comes to the boil and thickens. Strain into a clean bowl, add the butter and stir until the butter has melted and is incorporated into the mixture. Cover the surface with clingfilm/plastic wrap and leave to cool before refrigerating.

Whip the cream until it will hold soft peaks and fold into the chilled custard.

buttercream

125 g/1 stick unsalted butter, softened

250 g/1⅔ cups icing/confectioners' sugar, sifted

1 teaspoon vanilla, lemon, coffee or orange extract or rose water

Beat the butter until creamy and pale. Gradually add the sifted icing/confectioners' sugar, beating well until the buttercream is smooth. Add your chosen flavouring and mix well to combine. Use at room temperature.

white chocolate ganache

150 g/5 oz. white chocolate, finely chopped

5 tablespoons double/heavy cream

1 teaspoon vanilla extract

Put the chocolate in a small, heatproof bowl. Put the cream and vanilla extract in a small saucepan and heat until the cream has come to the boil. Pour the hot cream over the chopped chocolate and leave to melt for 1 minute. Stir until smooth then leave to cool. Cover and refrigerate until thickened.

mascarpone cream

Sweeten the required amount of mascarpone or whipped cream with icing/confectioners' or caster/superfine sugar. Add a drop of vanilla or coffee extract, citrus zest and juice, or even a splash of your preferred liqueur.

extra ideas

If you're stuck for time, you could simply fill your macarons with the best storebought jam, chocolate spread or toffee sauce. Or try swirling any of them into whipped cream, mascarpone or crème fraîche.

Here are a few quick filling suggestions:

° Fold lightly crushed raspberries or strawberries into whipped cream.

° Mix passion-fruit pulp with lemon curd.

° Fill each macaron with a small scoop of your favourite ice cream and serve with chocolate sauce or fresh fruit coulis.

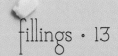

fillings · 13

matches made in heaven

Stuck for inspiration?
Try one of these
perfect pairings. Each
stack is made from
one flavour of shell,
with suggested fillings
from top to bottom.

coconut shells

from page 57, filled with:

apricot mascarpone (page 21)

caramelized banana (page 38)

passion-fruit ganache (page 46)

chocolate shells

from page 9, filled with:

salted caramel (page 37)

coffee cream (page 35)

peanut butter (page 54)

almond shells

from page 58, filled with:

white chocolate ganache
(page 13)

chocolate ganache (page 10)

gingerbread spice (page 51)

malted milk shells

from page 45, filled with:

hazelnut & chocolate ganache
(page 61)

storebought toffee sauce

almond praline (page 58)

creative combinations

Once you've mastered the technique for making basic macaron shells, you can start experimenting with different flavour combinations. You'll soon discover that there's no end to the fabulous matches you can create. Why not make up two different shells and a variety of three or four fillings and create an assortment box?

These are some of my favourite alternative combinations.

° Raspberry shells with white or dark chocolate ganache

° Vanilla shells with apricot or mango filling

° Pink and green shells with good-quality raspberry jam and whipped cream

° Chocolate and malted milk shells with coffee filling

° Coconut and banana shells with chocolate ganache

° Chocolate shells with gingerbread spice filling

° Lemon shells with fresh blueberry filling

fruit
& flowers

Try piping these macarons into delicate fingers instead of the usual round shapes and fill with blueberry purée, fresh blueberries and a delicate vanilla cream.

blueberry & vanilla

1 quantity Basic Macarons recipe (page 6)

purple food colouring paste

pink or purple sugar sprinkles

filling

300 g/3 cups blueberries

1 tablespoon granulated sugar

1 quantity Vanilla Cream (page 11)

2 solid baking sheets, lined with baking parchment

a piping bag, fitted with a star-shaped nozzle/tip

Prepare the Basic Macarons according to the recipe on page 6, adding purple food colouring paste to the meringue mixture in Step 4.

Pipe 6-cm/2½-inch-long fingers (instead of rounds) of mixture onto the prepared baking sheets. Tap the baking sheets sharply on the work surface, then scatter sugar sprinkles over the tops. Leave the macarons to rest for 15 minutes–1 hour.

Preheat the oven to 170°C (325°F) Gas 3.

Bake the macarons on the middle shelf of the preheated oven, one sheet at a time, for 10 minutes. Leave to cool on the baking sheet.

To make the filling, tip half the blueberries into a small saucepan, add the sugar and 1 tablespoon water and cook over medium heat until the berries soften and burst, then continue to cook until reduced and thickened to a jam-like consistency. Transfer to a nylon sieve/strainer, press through into a small bowl and set aside to cool.

Spread the filling over half the macaron shells and arrange the whole blueberries on top, spaced apart. Pipe the vanilla cream between the blueberries and top with the remaining macaron shells.

Decorate the top of these macarons with speckles of yellow and red liquid food colouring. When they're in season you could also purée fresh apricots for the filling.

apricot & almond

1 quantity Basic Macarons recipe (page 6)

yellow food colouring paste

red and yellow liquid food colouring

filling

150 g/1 cup ready-to-eat dried apricots

1 tablespoon lemon juice

1 tablespoon honey

2–3 tablespoons Amaretto or apricot brandy

4 generous tablespoons mascarpone

2 solid baking sheets, lined with baking parchment

a clean toothbrush

Start making the filling the day before making the macaron shells.

Roughly chop the apricots and place them in a saucepan with the lemon juice, honey and Amaretto or brandy. Heat gently but do not boil. Remove from the heat and leave the apricots to soak overnight until plump and juicy.

The next day, whiz the apricots and any remaining liquid in a food processor until they are as smooth as possible. Add the mascarpone and pulse just until incorporated. Spoon into a bowl, cover and refrigerate until needed.

Prepare the Basic Macarons according to the recipe on page 6, adding yellow food colouring paste to the meringue mixture in Step 4.

Pipe rounds of mixture onto the prepared baking sheets. Tap the baking sheets sharply on the work surface. Trickle a little red food colouring onto a saucer, then dip the clean toothbrush into it. Flick the bristles over the macarons so that they are flecked with red. Repeat with the yellow colouring. Leave the macarons to rest for 15 minutes–1 hour.

Preheat the oven to 170°C (325°F) Gas 3.

Bake the macarons on the middle shelf of the preheated oven, one sheet at a time, for 10 minutes. Leave to cool on the baking sheet.

Spread the filling over half the macaron shells and sandwich with the other half. Leave to rest for about 30 minutes before serving.

This is one of those flavours that creeps up on you after the first bite: first you taste the deep chocolatey-ness and then the blackcurrant sneaks in and takes over.

blackcurrant & chocolate

1 quantity Basic Macarons recipe (page 6)
purple food colouring paste

filling

125 g/1 generous cup fresh or frozen blackcurrants

1–2 tablespoons granulated sugar

1 tablespoon crème de cassis (blackcurrant liqueur)

100 ml/½ cup double/ heavy cream

½ tablespoon light muscovado/light brown sugar

100 g/3½ oz. dark/bittersweet chocolate, finely chopped

2 solid baking sheets, lined with baking parchment

Prepare the filling before making the macaron shells.

Tip the blackcurrants into a small saucepan, add the granulated sugar and 1 tablespoon water and cook over low heat until the currants are very soft and juicy. Remove from the heat and press through a nylon sieve/strainer into a bowl. Taste and add a little more sugar, if needed. Return the purée to the pan along with the crème de cassis and cook over low heat, stirring constantly, until reduced to 4 tablespoons.

Put the cream and muscovado/brown sugar in a small saucepan and bring to the boil. Tip the chocolate into a heatproof bowl, pour the hot cream over it and mix until smooth. Stir in the blackcurrant purée and leave until cool, then cover and refrigerate until ready to use.

Prepare the Basic Macarons according to the recipe on page 6, adding purple food colouring paste to the meringue mixture in Step 4.

Pipe rounds of mixture onto the prepared baking sheets. Tap the baking sheets sharply on the work surface and leave the macarons to rest for 15 minutes–1 hour.

Preheat the oven to 170°C (325°F) Gas 3.

Bake the macarons on the middle shelf of the preheated oven, one sheet at a time, for 10 minutes. Leave to cool on the baking sheet.

Spread the filling over half the macaron shells and sandwich with the other half. Leave to rest for about 30 minutes before serving.

You could make boxes of these dainty rose-infused macarons in varying shades of pink – perfect for an afternoon tea with the girls.

rose

1 quantity Basic Macarons recipe (page 6)

pink food colouring paste

½ teaspoon rose water

1 tablespoon rose sprinkles or crystallized rose petals, finely chopped

filling

1 quantity Buttercream (page 11, using ½ teaspoon rose water)

2 solid baking sheets, lined with baking parchment

a piping bag, fitted with a star-shaped nozzle/tip

Prepare the Basic Macarons according to the recipe on page 6, adding pink food colouring paste and the rose water to the meringue mixture in Step 4.

Pipe rounds of mixture onto the prepared baking sheets. Tap the baking sheets sharply on the work surface, then scatter rose sprinkles or petals over the tops. Leave the macarons to rest for 15 minutes–1 hour.

Preheat the oven to 170°C (325°F) Gas 3.

Bake the macarons on the middle shelf of the preheated oven, one sheet at a time, for 10 minutes. Leave to cool on the baking sheet.

Fill the piping bag with the rose-flavoured buttercream and pipe it onto half the macaron shells. Sandwich with the other half and leave to rest for about 30 minutes before serving.

Reminiscent of boxes of violet fondant cream chocolates, all the elements are here but in a macaron. Consult the stockists on page 4 for violet flavouring.

violet creams

1 quantity Basic Macarons recipe (page 6)
1–2 teaspoons violet flavouring (see page 4)
purple food colouring paste

filling

½ quantity Chocolate Ganache (page 10)
½ quantity White Chocolate Ganache (page 13)
2 solid baking sheets, lined with baking parchment
2 piping bags, fitted with star-shaped nozzles/tips

makes about 30

Prepare the Basic Macarons according to the recipe on page 6, adding the violet flavouring and some purple food colouring paste to the meringue mixture in Step 4.

Pipe 2.5-cm/1-inch rounds of mixture onto the prepared baking sheets. Tap the baking sheets sharply on the work surface and leave the macarons to rest for 15 minutes–1 hour.

Preheat the oven to 170°C (325°F) Gas 3.

Bake the macarons on the middle shelf of the preheated oven, one sheet at a time, for 7 minutes. Leave to cool on the baking sheet.

Fill each piping bag with the prepared ganaches. Pipe one ganache over one-quarter of the macaron shells and sandwich together with another quarter. Repeat with the other ganache and the remaining macaron shells. Leave to rest for about 30 minutes before serving.

Here's a classic autumnal fruit combination that works perfectly in macarons not only because it tastes great, but also because the colours complement each other.

apple & blackberry

1 quantity Basic Macarons recipe (page 6)
purple food colouring paste
green food colouring paste

filling

4 small dessert apples, e.g. Cox's or Winesap

1 tablespoon granulated sugar

freshly squeezed juice of ½ lemon

125 g/1 cup blackberries

100 ml/½ cup double/ heavy cream

2 solid baking sheets, lined with baking parchment

a piping bag, fitted with a star-shaped nozzle/tip

Prepare the filling before you make the macaron shells.

Peel, core and roughly chop the apples and place in a medium saucepan with the sugar and lemon juice. Cover and cook over low heat until the fruit has started to soften, stirring from time to time. Add the blackberries and continue to cook for a further 10–15 minutes until the fruit has reduced to a thick purée. Remove from the heat and press through a nylon sieve/strainer into a small bowl. Taste and add a little more sugar, if needed.

Prepare the Basic Macarons according to the recipe on page 6, but when you get to Step 4, divide the mixture between 2 bowls and add purple food colouring paste to one bowl and green food colouring paste to the other.

Pipe 20 rounds of each colour of mixture onto each prepared baking sheet. Tap the baking sheets sharply on the work surface and leave the macarons to rest for 15 minutes–1 hour.

Preheat the oven to 170°C (325°F) Gas 3.

Bake the macarons on the middle shelf of the preheated oven, one sheet at a time, for 10 minutes. Leave to cool on the baking sheet.

Lightly whip the cream. Spread the fruit filling onto the purple macaron shells. Fill the piping bag with the whipped cream and pipe it onto the green shells. Sandwich the two together and leave to rest for about 30 minutes before serving.

The taste of summer in a macaron! These are somewhere between British scones and a Victoria sandwich and are all the better for using homemade strawberry jam.

strawberries & cream

1 quantity Basic Macarons recipe (page 6)
1 vanilla pod/bean, split lengthways
red or pink edible glitter

filling

4 tablespoons best-quality strawberry jam
1 quantity Vanilla Cream (page 11)

2 solid baking sheets, lined with baking parchment

a piping bag, fitted with a plain nozzle/tip

Prepare the Basic Macarons according to the recipe on page 6, scraping the vanilla seeds from the split pod/bean into the meringue mixture in Step 4.

Pipe rounds of mixture onto the prepared baking sheets. Tap the baking sheets sharply on the work surface, then scatter glitter over the tops. Leave the macarons to rest for 15 minutes–1 hour.

Preheat the oven to 170°C (325°F) Gas 3.

Bake the macarons on the middle shelf of the preheated oven, one sheet at a time, for 10 minutes. Leave to cool on the baking sheet.

Take one half of the macaron shells and spread about ½ teaspoon strawberry jam onto each one. Fill the piping bag with the Vanilla Cream and pipe it onto the remaining shells. Sandwich together with the jammy macarons and leave to rest for about 30 minutes before serving.

I love fruit curds and this raspberry and passion-fruit one used as a filling is no exception. You may need to add food colouring to it to make it a more punchy pink.

raspberry & passion fruit

1 quantity Basic Macarons recipe (page 6)

red or pink food colouring paste

filling

125 g/1 cup raspberries

2 passion fruit

3 egg yolks

50 g/¼ cup caster/superfine sugar

50 g/3 tablespoons unsalted butter, diced

2 solid baking sheets, lined with baking parchment

Prepare the Basic Macarons according to the recipe on page 6, adding red or pink food colouring paste to the meringue mixture in Step 4.

Pipe rounds of mixture onto the prepared baking sheets. Tap the baking sheets sharply on the work surface and leave the macarons to rest for 15 minutes–1 hour.

Preheat the oven to 170°C (325°F) Gas 3.

Bake the macarons on the middle shelf of the preheated oven, one sheet at a time, for 10 minutes. Leave to cool on the baking sheet.

To make the filling, whiz the raspberries in a food processor, then press through a nylon sieve/strainer into a medium heatproof bowl. Cut the passion fruit in half, scoop the seeds and juice into the raspberry bowl and add the egg yolks, sugar and unsalted butter. Set the bowl over a pan of simmering water and cook for about 10–15 minutes, stirring from time to time until the curd has thickened and will coat the back of a spoon. Strain into a clean bowl and add a tiny amount of red or pink food colouring paste if you need to accentuate the raspberry colour. Cover the surface of the curd with clingfilm/plastic wrap and leave to cool before refrigerating for a couple of hours.

Spread the filling over half the macaron shells and sandwich with the other half. Leave to rest for about 30 minutes before serving.

coffee, caramel & chocolate

Pipe the filling into these delicate coffee-flavoured macarons in an extra-thick layer. Alternatively, you could fill the shells with Chocolate Ganache (see page 10) flavoured with coffee extract to create mocha macarons.

cappuccino

1 quantity Basic Macarons recipe (page 6)

2 teaspoons coffee extract or 2 teaspoons instant coffee granules dissolved in 1 teaspoon boiling water

brown food colouring paste

cocoa powder, for dusting

filling

1 quantity Vanilla Cream (page 11)

1 teaspoon coffee extract

2 solid baking sheets, lined with baking parchment

a piping bag, fitted with a plain nozzle/tip

Prepare the Basic Macarons according to the recipe on page 6, adding the coffee extract and brown food colouring paste to the meringue mixture in Step 4.

Pipe rounds of mixture onto the prepared baking sheets. Tap the baking sheets sharply on the work surface, then lightly dust cocoa powder over the tops. Leave the macarons to rest for 15 minutes–1 hour.

Preheat the oven to 170°C (325°F) Gas 3.

Bake the macarons on the middle shelf of the preheated oven, one sheet at a time, for 10 minutes. Leave to cool on the baking sheet.

To make the filling, prepare the Vanilla Cream according to the recipe on page 11 and stir in the coffee extract. Fill the piping bag with the coffee cream and pipe it onto half the macaron shells. Pipe two or three layers of filling to make an extra-generous filling. Sandwich with the other half of the shells and leave to rest for about 30 minutes before serving.

Salted caramel seems to be the flavour of the moment, and the combination works like a dream sandwiched in the middle of macarons.

salted caramel

1 quantity Basic Macarons recipe (page 6)

1 teaspoon vanilla extract

filling

75 g/⅓ cup caster/superfine sugar

75 g/⅓ cup light muscovado/light brown sugar

50 g/3 tablespoons unsalted butter

100 ml/½ cup double/heavy cream

½ teaspoon sea salt flakes

2 solid baking sheets, lined with baking parchment

Prepare the Basic Macarons according to the recipe on page 6, adding the vanilla extract to the meringue mixture in Step 4.

Pipe rounds of mixture onto the prepared baking sheets. Tap the baking sheets sharply on the work surface and leave the macarons to rest for 15 minutes–1 hour.

Preheat the oven to 170°C (325°F) Gas 3.

Bake the macarons on the middle shelf of the preheated oven, one sheet at a time, for 10 minutes. Leave to cool on the baking sheet.

To make the filling, put the caster/superfine sugar and 2 tablespoons water in a small saucepan over low heat and let the sugar dissolve completely. Bring to the boil, then cook until the syrup turns to an amber-coloured caramel. Remove from the heat and add the muscovado/brown sugar, butter and cream. Stir to dissolve, then return to the low heat and simmer for 3–4 minutes, until the caramel has thickened and will coat the back of a spoon. Remove from the heat, add the salt, pour into a bowl and leave until completely cold and thick.

Spread the filling over half the macaron shells and sandwich with the other half. Leave to rest for about 30 minutes before serving.

For this grown-up version of the family favourite, bananas, caramel, chocolate and cream compete in a divine filling.

banoffee

1 quantity Basic Macarons recipe (page 6)

yellow food colouring paste

2–3 tablespoons finely chopped dried banana chips

filling

75 g/⅓ cup caster/ superfine sugar

1 large or 2 small, ripe bananas, peeled and thickly sliced

100 ml/½ cup double/ heavy cream

1 quantity Chocolate Ganache (page 10)

2 solid baking sheets, lined with baking parchment

a piping bag, fitted with a plain nozzle/tip

Prepare the Basic Macarons according to the recipe on page 6, adding yellow food colouring paste to the meringue mixture in Step 4.

Pipe rounds of mixture onto the prepared baking sheets. Tap the baking sheets sharply on the work surface, then scatter the chopped banana chips over the tops. Leave the macarons to rest for 15 minutes–1 hour.

Preheat the oven to 170°C (325°F) Gas 3.

Bake the macarons on the middle shelf of the preheated oven, one sheet at a time, for 10 minutes. Leave to cool on the baking sheet.

To make the filling, put the sugar and 1–2 tablespoons water in a small saucepan over low heat and let the sugar dissolve completely. Increase the heat and bring to the boil, then cook until the syrup turns to an amber-coloured caramel. Remove from the heat and add the sliced bananas. Stir to coat and soften in the caramel. Tip the contents of the pan into a food processor and blend until smooth, then set aside to cool completely.

Lightly whip the cream. Spread the Chocolate Ganache onto half the macaron shells. Fill the piping bag with the whipped cream and pipe a circle of it onto the remaining macaron shells, then spoon the banoffee sauce into the middle. Sandwich the macarons together and leave to rest for about 30 minutes before serving.

Lightly dip the bristles of a clean toothbrush into liquid food colouring. Using your fingertips, "flick" the bristles over uncooked macarons for a Jackson Pollock effect.

white chocolate & raspberry

1 quantity Basic Macarons recipe (page 6)

1 teaspoon vanilla extract

red liquid food colouring

filling

1 quantity White Chocolate Ganache (page 13)

200 g/1½ cups raspberries

2 solid baking sheets, lined with baking parchment

a clean toothbrush

a piping bag, fitted with a star-shaped nozzle/tip

Prepare the Basic Macarons according to the recipe on page 6, adding the vanilla extract to the meringue mixture in Step 4.

Pipe rounds of mixture onto the prepared baking sheets. Tap the baking sheets sharply on the work surface. Trickle a little red food colouring onto a saucer, then dip the clean toothbrush into it. Flick the bristles over the macarons so that they are flecked with red. Leave the macarons to rest for 15 minutes–1 hour.

Preheat the oven to 170°C (325°F) Gas 3.

Bake the macarons on the middle shelf of the preheated oven, one sheet at a time, for 10 minutes. Leave to cool on the baking sheet.

Fill the piping bag with the White Chocolate Ganache and pipe 4 rosettes near the edge of half the macaron shells. Place a raspberry between each rosette and sandwich with the remaining macaron shells. Leave to rest for 30 minutes before serving.

Black Forest gâteau in a macaron. Dried cherries are one of my favourite baking ingredients – soaked in sweet booze, they are a sublime partner for rich chocolate.

chocolate & cherry

1 quantity Chocolate Macarons recipe (page 9)

filling

75 g/½ cup dried sour cherries

1–2 tablespoons cherry brandy

1 tablespoon granulated sugar

1 quantity Chocolate Ganache (page 10)

100 ml/½ cup double/ heavy cream

2 solid baking sheets, lined with baking parchment

Prepare the filling before you make the macaron shells.

Put the dried cherries in a small saucepan with the brandy, sugar and 2 tablespoons water. Set over low heat and bring to just below boiling point. Remove from the heat and leave the cherries to soak for at least 2 hours. They will absorb the liquid and become plump and juicy.

Meanwhile, put the Chocolate Ganache in the fridge to thicken.

Prepare the Chocolate Macarons according to the recipe on page 9.

Pipe rounds of mixture onto the prepared baking sheets. Tap the baking sheets sharply on the work surface and leave the macarons to rest for 15 minutes–1 hour.

Preheat the oven to 170°C (325°F) Gas 3.

Bake the macarons on the middle shelf of the preheated oven, one sheet at a time, for 10 minutes. Leave to cool on the baking sheet.

Tip the soaked cherries and any remaining juice into a food processor and blend until well chopped but not smooth. Lightly whip the cream and fold it into the chopped cherry mixture.

Spread the Chocolate Ganache onto half the macaron shells. Spread cherry cream onto the remaining macaron shells and sandwich the two together. Leave to rest for 30 minutes before serving.

Serve these macarons with a dipping sauce of warm, deeply rich, malted hot chocolate. Swap your evening cup of cocoa for this deliciously decadent treat.

malted chocolate

1 quantity Basic Macarons recipe (page 6)

2 tablespoons malted milk powder

cocoa powder, for dusting

filling

1 quantity Chocolate Ganache (page 10)

1 tablespoon malted milk powder

2 solid baking sheets, lined with baking parchment

Prepare the Basic Macarons according to the recipe on page 6, adding the malted milk powder to the food processor in Step 1.

Pipe rounds of mixture onto the prepared baking sheets. Tap the baking sheets sharply on the work surface, then lightly dust cocoa powder over the tops. Leave the macarons to rest for 15 minutes–1 hour.

Preheat the oven to 170°C (325°F) Gas 3.

Bake the macarons on the middle shelf of the preheated oven, one sheet at a time, for 10 minutes. Leave to cool on the baking sheet.

To make the filling, prepare the Chocolate Ganache according to the recipe on page 10, adding the malted milk powder to the hot cream.

Spread the filling over half the macaron shells and sandwich with the other half. Leave to rest for about 30 minutes before serving.

First you taste the chocolate, and then the passion-fruit flavour hits you in an unexpected and delicious way. These are quite possibly my favourite macarons.

chocolate & passion fruit

1 quantity Basic Macarons recipe (page 6)

yellow food colouring paste

chocolate sprinkles or flakes

filling

6 passion fruit

1 quantity Chocolate Ganache (page 10)

2 solid baking sheets, lined with baking parchment

Prepare the Basic Macarons according to the recipe on page 6, adding yellow food colouring paste to the meringue mixture in Step 4.

Pipe rounds of mixture onto the prepared baking sheets. Tap the baking sheets sharply on the work surface, then scatter the chocolate sprinkles over the tops. Leave the macarons to rest for 15 minutes–1 hour.

Preheat the oven to 170°C (325°F) Gas 3.

Bake the macarons on the middle shelf of the preheated oven, one sheet at a time, for 10 minutes. Leave to cool on the baking sheet.

To make the filling, cut the passion fruit in half and scoop the seeds and juice into a nylon sieve/strainer set over a small saucepan. Using the back of spoon, press the pulp through the sieve – you should end up with about 4–5 tablespoons of juice. Set the pan over low–medium heat and bring slowly to the boil. Cook gently until the juice has reduced by half and you have about 1–2 tablespoons thick passion-fruit juice remaining.

Stir the thick passion-fruit juice into the Chocolate Ganache, then spread over half the macaron shells. Sandwich with the remaining macaron shells and leave to rest for 30 minutes before serving.

Look for edible gold sugar stars at sugarcraft suppliers (see page 4) to scatter liberally over the top of these macarons — perfect for the festive season.

caramel & nutmeg ganache

1 quantity Basic Macarons recipe (page 6)
brown food colouring paste
freshly grated nutmeg
edible gold stars

filling

75 g/⅓ cup caster/ superfine sugar
200 ml/¾ cup double/ heavy cream
150 g/5 oz. dark/bittersweet chocolate, finely chopped
¼ teaspoon freshly grated nutmeg

2 solid baking sheets, lined with baking parchment

Prepare the filling before making the macaron shells.

Put the sugar and 1 tablespoon water in a small saucepan over low–medium heat and let the sugar dissolve completely. Increase the heat and bring to the boil, then cook until the syrup turns to an amber-coloured caramel. Remove the pan from the heat and pour in the cream. Stir until smooth, returning to a low heat if necessary to re-melt the caramel.

Tip the chopped chocolate into a heatproof bowl, pour the hot caramel cream over it, add the nutmeg and stir until smooth. Leave to cool, then cover and refrigerate until needed.

Prepare the Basic Macarons according to the recipe on page 6, adding brown food colouring paste and a generous grating of nutmeg to the meringue mixture in Step 4.

Pipe rounds of mixture onto the prepared baking sheets. Tap the baking sheets sharply on the work surface, then scatter gold stars over the tops. Leave the macarons to rest for 15 minutes–1 hour.

Preheat the oven to 170°C (325°F) Gas 3.

Bake the macarons on the middle shelf of the preheated oven, one sheet at a time, for 10 minutes. Leave to cool on the baking sheet.

Spread the filling over half the macaron shells and sandwich with the other half. Leave to rest for about 30 minutes before serving.

nuts & spice
& all things nice

Here are all the flavours of Christmas in one crisp mouthful. Warm spices and caramel are combined in a macaron that's somewhat similar to gingerbread.

gingerbread spice

1 quantity Basic Macarons recipe (page 6)
1 teaspoon ground cinnamon
1 teaspoon ground ginger
a pinch of ground cloves
a pinch of freshly grated nutmeg

filling

1 quantity Buttercream (page 11) or 150 g/⅔ cup mascarpone
1 big tablespoon dulce de leche
1 tablespoon finely chopped stem ginger
½ teaspoon ground cinnamon

2 solid baking sheets, lined with baking parchment

Prepare the Basic Macarons according to the recipe on page 6, adding the cinnamon, ginger, cloves and nutmeg to the food processor in Step 1.

Pipe rounds of mixture onto the prepared baking sheets. Tap the baking sheets sharply on the work surface and leave the macarons to rest for 15 minutes–1 hour.

Preheat the oven to 170°C (325°F) Gas 3.

Bake the macarons on the middle shelf of the preheated oven, one sheet at a time, for 10 minutes. Leave to cool on the baking sheet.

To make the filling, put the Buttercream or mascarpone in a small bowl and stir in the dulce de leche, stem ginger and cinnamon.

Spread the filling over half the macaron shells and sandwich with the other half. Leave to rest for about 30 minutes before serving.

The taste of the tropics! If you can find them, use super-sweet, flavoursome Alphonso mangoes.

coconut & mango

1 quantity Basic Macarons
recipe (page 6)
2 tablespoons desiccated
coconut
yellow food colouring paste

filling

1 ripe mango
1 tablespoon palm sugar or
light brown sugar
1 tablespoon dark rum
100 g/3½ oz. white
chocolate, finely chopped
freshly squeezed lime juice,
to taste

*2 solid baking sheets,
lined with baking parchment*

Prepare the Basic Macarons according to the recipe on page 6, adding the desiccated coconut to the food processor in Step 1. Then add yellow food colouring paste to the meringue mixture in Step 4.

Pipe rounds of mixture onto the prepared baking sheets. Tap the baking sheets sharply on the work surface and leave the macarons to rest for 15 minutes–1 hour.

Preheat the oven to 170°C (325°F) Gas 3.

Bake the macarons on the middle shelf of the preheated oven, one sheet at a time, for 10 minutes. Leave to cool on the baking sheet.

To make the filling, slice the cheeks off the mango, score the flesh into dice and cut away from the skin. Tip the flesh into a small saucepan with the sugar and rum. Cook over low–medium heat until the mango is very soft and starting to caramelize. Remove from the heat and leave to cool slightly, then add the white chocolate and whiz in the food processor until smooth. Add squeezed lime juice to taste – you will probably only need 1 teaspoonful to balance the flavours.

Scoop the mango filling into a bowl and leave to cool before covering and refrigerating until ready to use.

Spread the filling over half the macaron shells and sandwich with the other half. Leave to rest for about 30 minutes before serving.

I am a recent convert to this flavour combination – it shouldn't work but somehow it does. The homemade peanut butter really does make all the difference.

peanut butter & raspberry

2 tablespoons shelled, skinned and unsalted peanuts

1 quantity Basic Macarons recipe (page 6)

extra peanuts, finely chopped, for sprinkling

pink sugar sprinkles

filling

75 g/½ cup shelled, skinned and unsalted peanuts

1 tablespoon icing/confectioners' sugar

3 tablespoons sweetened condensed milk

2 tablespoons unsalted butter

a pinch of salt

4 tablespoons raspberry jam

2 solid baking sheets, lined with baking parchment

makes about 30

Very finely chop the peanuts in a food processor.

Prepare the Basic Macarons according to the recipe on page 6, adding the finely chopped peanuts to the food processor in Step 1.

Pipe 2.5-cm/1-inch rounds of mixture onto the prepared baking sheets. Tap the baking sheets sharply on the work surface, then sprinkle the finely chopped peanuts over the tops of half the macaron shells and sugar sprinkles over the other half. Leave the macarons to rest for 15 minutes–1 hour.

Preheat the oven to 170°C (325°F) Gas 3.

Bake the macarons on the middle shelf of the preheated oven, one sheet at a time, for 7 minutes. Leave to cool on the baking sheet. Leave the oven on.

To make the filling, put the peanuts in a roasting pan and toast in the oven for 5 minutes, or until golden. Remove from the oven and leave to cool for 2–3 minutes before finely chopping in the food processor. Add the sugar, condensed milk, butter and salt and pulse again until the mixture turns to peanut butter.

Spread the peanut butter onto half the macaron shells. Spread the raspberry jam onto the remaining macaron shells and sandwich the two together. Leave to rest for 30 minutes before serving.

The addition of coconut to macaron shells makes them just a hint more delicious, if that's possible.

coconut & chocolate

1 quantity Basic Macarons recipe (page 6)

3 tablespoons desiccated coconut

filling

150 ml/⅔ cup double/heavy cream

1 quantity Chocolate Ganache (page 10)

2 solid baking sheets, lined with baking parchment

Prepare the Basic Macarons according to the recipe on page 6, adding 2 tablespoons of the desiccated coconut to the food processor in Step 1.

Pipe rounds of mixture onto the prepared baking sheets. Tap the baking sheets sharply on the work surface, then scatter the remaining tablespoon of desiccated coconut over the tops. Leave the macarons to rest for 15 minutes–1 hour.

Preheat the oven to 170°C (325°F) Gas 3.

Bake the macarons on the middle shelf of the preheated oven, one sheet at a time, for 10 minutes. Leave to cool on the baking sheet.

To make the filling, lightly whip the cream. Spread the cream onto half the macaron shells. Spread the Chocolate Ganache onto the remaining macaron shells and sandwich the two together. Leave to rest for 30 minutes before serving.

I love caramel in all its forms, and when mixed with almonds, it's a match made in heaven. Add whipped cream and you've got yourself a very delicious macaron.

almond praline

1 quantity Basic Macarons recipe (page 6)

2 tablespoons slivered almonds, chopped

1 tablespoon icing/confectioners' sugar

filling

50 g/⅓ cup blanched almonds

50 g/¼ cup caster/superfine sugar

125 ml/½ cup double/heavy cream

3 solid baking sheets

Prepare the filling before you make the macaron shells. Preheat the oven to 180°C (350°F) Gas 4. Line 2 baking sheets with parchment paper and oil the third sheet with sunflower oil.

Tip the blanched almonds into a small roasting pan and toast in the preheated oven for about 5 minutes. Leave to cool slightly.

Put the sugar and 1 tablespoon water in a small saucepan over low–medium heat and let the sugar dissolve completely. Increase the heat and bring to the boil, then cook until the syrup turns to an amber-coloured caramel. Add the toasted almonds and, working quickly, stir to coat in the caramel. Tip the praline mixture onto the oiled baking sheet and leave until completely cold. Break the cold, hard praline into pieces and whiz in the food processor until finely ground. Store in an airtight container until ready to use.

Prepare the Basic Macarons according to the recipe on page 6.

Pipe rounds of mixture onto the lined baking sheets. Tap the baking sheets sharply on the work surface, then scatter the chopped slivered almonds and icing/confectioners' sugar over the tops. Leave the macarons to rest for 15 minutes–1 hour.

Preheat the oven to 170°C (325°F) Gas 3.

Bake the macarons on the middle shelf of the preheated oven, one sheet at a time, for 10 minutes. Leave to cool on the baking sheet. Lightly whip the cream and stir in the ground praline. Spread the filling over half the macaron shells and sandwich with the other half. Leave to rest for 30 minutes before serving.

These mini-macarons are filled with a homemade chocolate and hazelnut spread — an altogether more sophisticated version of the storebought variety.

hazelnut & chocolate

1 quantity Basic Macarons recipe (page 6, but follow instructions in method, right)

50 g/⅓ cup ground hazelnuts

1 tablespoon cocoa powder

filling

35 g/¼ cup blanched hazelnuts

4 tablespoons sweetened condensed milk

50 g/2 oz. dark/bittersweet chocolate, finely chopped

1 tablespoon double/heavy cream

a pinch of salt

2 solid baking sheets, lined with baking parchment

makes about 30

Prepare the Basic Macarons according to the recipe on page 6 but use only 50 g/⅓ cup ground almonds. In Step 1, add 50 g/⅓ cup ground hazelnuts and 1 tablespoon cocoa powder to the food processor with the other ingredients. Continue with the recipe.

Pipe 2.5-cm/1-inch rounds of mixture onto the prepared baking sheets. Tap the baking sheets sharply on the work surface and leave the macarons to rest for 15 minutes–1 hour.

Preheat the oven to 170°C (325°F) Gas 3.

Bake the macarons on the middle shelf of the preheated oven, one sheet at a time, for 7 minutes. Leave to cool on the baking sheet. Leave the oven on.

To make the filling, tip the blanched hazelnuts into a small roasting pan and toast in the preheated oven for about 7 minutes. Leave to cool slightly, then whiz in a food processor until very finely chopped and starting to clump together.

Melt the condensed milk and chocolate together in a microwave or in a small saucepan over low heat. When it is melted and smooth, pour into the food processor with the ground hazelnuts and blend until smooth. Add the cream and salt and mix again. Leave to thicken slightly.

Spread the filling over half the macaron shells and sandwich with the other half. Leave to rest for 30 minutes before serving.

If you thought after-dinner mints were irresistible, try these and you'll be converted. Bake a box of them and bring to a dinner party as a gift.

mint & chocolate

1 quantity Basic Macarons recipe (page 6)
green food colouring paste

filling

25 g/1 oz. fresh mint leaves
40 g/3 tablespoons caster/superfine sugar
150 g/5 oz. dark/bittersweet chocolate, finely chopped
2 solid baking sheets, lined with baking parchment

Prepare the filling before you make the macaron shells.

Lightly crush the mint leaves between your hands and place in a small saucepan with the sugar and 100 ml/½ cup water. Slowly bring to the boil so that the sugar dissolves, then simmer gently for about 3 minutes. Remove from the heat and set aside to infuse for at least 1 hour.

Tip the chocolate into a heatproof bowl. Bring the mint syrup back to the boil, then strain into the chopped chocolate. Stir until melted and smooth. Leave to cool and thicken slightly before using.

Prepare the Basic Macarons according to the recipe on page 6, adding green food colouring paste to the meringue mixture in Step 4.

Pipe rounds of mixture onto the prepared baking sheets. Tap the baking sheets sharply on the work surface and leave the macarons to rest for 15 minutes–1 hour.

Preheat the oven to 170°C (325°F) Gas 3.

Bake the macarons on the middle shelf of the preheated oven, one sheet at a time, for 10 minutes. Leave to cool on the baking sheet.

Spread the filling over half the macaron shells and sandwich with the other half. Leave to rest for 30 minutes before serving.

index